BEHIND THE SMILE

Unveiling Jennifer Aniston's Inspiring
Story

WILLIAM B DRUMMOND

Behind The Smile

Unveiling Jennifer Aniston's Inspiring Story.

By

William B Drummond

Behind the smile

Behind the smile

TABLE OF CONTENTS

and life lessons along the way. Discover the unwavering determination that propelled Jennifer from her early days as a struggling actress to becoming a household name. Gain a deeper understanding of the challenges she faced in an industry known for its fierce competition, and how she overcame obstacles with grace and resilience. We'll explore the transformative power of her iconic role as Rachel Green in the hit television series "Friends" and the indelible mark it left on pop culture. We'll also examine her diverse filmography, ranging from romantic comedies to dramatic roles, and how she continually reinvents herself as an actress of unparalleled versatility.

Beyond her professional achievements, "Behind the Smile" delves into the philanthropic endeavors that are dear to Jennifer's heart, shedding light on her passion for empowering women, advocating for various causes, and promoting mental health awareness.

Behind the smile

This book is a tribute to a true Hollywood icon, an invitation to delve into the depths of her extraordinary life, and an opportunity to glean valuable life lessons from her experiences. Prepare to be captivated, educated, and inspired as we uncover the story of Jennifer Aniston, a woman whose radiant smile is just the beginning of her incredible tale.

CHAPTER 1

The Mysterious Star: Contextualizing Jennifer Aniston's enthralling journey

Childhood Years

On February 11, 1969, Jennifer Joanna Aniston was born in Sherman Oaks, Los Angeles, California. Her mother Nancy Dow was an actress and model, and her father John Aniston was a well-known soap opera actor. She was raised in a Hollywood household. Her early exposure to the entertainment world was likely influenced by the occupations of her parents.

Aniston discovered her love for acting while attending the Fiorello H. LaGuardia High School of Music, Art, and Performing Arts in New York City.

She followed her passion in Los Angeles after college, doing a variety of part-time jobs and going to auditions. Aniston's career took a turn for the better in 1994 when she was employed to play Rachel Green on the popular television comedy "Friends." Aniston and her co-stars were propelled to worldwide popularity by the program, which was produced by David Crane and Marta Kauffman and became a cultural sensation. Audiences all across the globe were moved by Aniston's depiction of the stylish and endearing Rachel. She won over millions of followers with her charisma, relatability, and humorous timing. Aniston won several accolades and honors throughout her ten-year tenure on "Friends," including an Emmy and a Golden Globe. As a result of her $1 million per episode pay in the latter seasons, she rose to become one of the highest-paid television actresses of all time. In addition to making Aniston a household celebrity, the show's popularity gave her a stage on which to demonstrate her acting skills and range. After "Friends" ended in 2004, Aniston made the switch to cinema, showcasing her versatility outside of the comedy medium. She acted in a range of genres, including dramas, romantic comedies, and independent movies. She has acted in some well-known movies, such as "Marley & Me," "The Break-Up," "Along Came Polly," "Cake," and "The Morning Show." Aniston's uncanny ability to transition between tragic and humorous parts cemented her reputation as a talented actor.

Aniston has pursued a producing career in addition to performing. In 2008, she and Kristin Hahn founded their own production business,

Behind the smile

Echo Films. She has contributed to the planning and execution of several projects via Echo Films, including the much-praised movie "Cake," in which she also appeared. Aniston's producing work highlights her dedication to promoting different narratives and assisting up-and-coming talent in the field.

Aniston has received a lot of media attention for her personal life in addition to her professional achievements. Her high-profile marriage to Brad Pitt and subsequent divorce made headlines throughout the globe. She has, nevertheless, been able to maintain a tough and secluded demeanor while concentrating on her career and charitable initiatives.

Aniston has received praise throughout her career for both her acting prowess as well as her classic beauty and sense of fashion. "The Rachel," her famous hairdo from "Friends," became a worldwide craze and was imitated by numerous others. Aniston has been on the pages of several fashion publications, and she is praised for her dedication to timeless and refined style.

Aniston has embraced the digital age in recent years, joining Instagram and gaining millions of followers in no time. Fans have been able to get glimpses into her personal life and behind-the-scenes activities from her projects thanks to her social media presence.

Her genuineness and humor have made her popular with a younger audience and cemented her place as a beloved and significant figure in pop culture. Aniston's trajectory after "Friends" has been characterized by her aptitude for bridging the gap between television and movies. Successful romantic comedies like "Marley & Me" and "The Break-Up," which highlighted her comic timing and on-screen chemistry with co-stars, helped her establish her box-office appeal. Her reputation as a leading woman in Hollywood was cemented by these parts. Aniston didn't stick to a single genre, however. She also accepted difficult dramatic parts that showed off her breadth and depth as a performer. She received positive reviews for her role in the movie "Cake" and was nominated for prizes including the Golden Globe and the Screen Actors Guild Award. She was able to take on challenging roles in this role, showcasing her talent for drama.

She has aggressively pursued her interest in producing via her firm Echo Films in addition to her acting career. She has looked for projects that tell interesting stories and provide underrepresented voices in the business a chance to be heard. Her involvement in the development of movies like "The Switch" and "Dumplin'" demonstrates her dedication to supporting varied tales and elevating up-and-coming talent.

Beyond her work in front of and behind the camera, Aniston has a significant influence. She has supported charitable organizations and given back to the community by using her platform. She has worked with institutions including Stand Up To Cancer, the American Foundation for

Behind the smile

AIDS Research, and St. Jude Children's Research Hospital. Aniston's charitable activities demonstrate her desire to have a good effect on society and use her influence for significant change.

Aniston has managed to remain genuine and graceful despite the demands and scrutiny that come with being a public person. She has persevered through personal struggles and keeps putting her health and personal development first. Fans who like her strength and relatability have taken a shine to Aniston because of her ability to stay grounded and true to herself. Aniston's lasting popularity has also been aided by her ageless beauty and trademark style. She has established herself as a fashion star because of her chic red-carpet attire and carefree off-duty appearance. Through partnerships with fashion companies, her appearances on magazine covers, and the way her style continues to shape trends, her effect on the industry is evident. Aniston has embraced social media in recent years, especially Instagram, where she engages with her followers and posts snippets of her life. She has become a social media star because of her interesting and entertaining postings, which have also given her the chance to meet a new generation of fans. Aniston's online persona exhibits her honesty and openness to use fresh venues for audience engagement.

The fascinating career of Jennifer Aniston is evidence of her skill, tenacity, and capacity to develop as an artist. She has had an enduring impact on popular culture and the entertainment business, beginning with her breakout performance as Rachel Green on "Friends" and continuing with her successful film career, charitable work, and ageless influence. Aniston's path acts as motivation for budding performers and a reminder of the importance of pursuing your passions with a genuine sense of who you are to succeed and leave a lasting impression.

Examining the fascination and mystery contained in her beautiful smile

Investigating Jennifer Aniston's smile's attraction exposes not just its alluring beauty but also the mystery and warmth it conceals. Aniston's grin has grown to be one of her most recognizable traits, captivating viewers all around the globe and adding to her timeless appeal. Aniston's grin is one of the most noticeable features because of how happy and contagious it is. Her eyes shine

Behind the smile

with happiness when she smiles, and her whole face becomes radiant. People are drawn in right away by the genuine warmth and optimism it radiates. Her smile can elevate people's emotions and give them a feeling of security.

The charm of Aniston's grin is found in its sincerity. It is an outward manifestation of her inner pleasure and happiness, which can be seen in her outward demeanor. She has remained approachable and personable throughout her career, and her grin is proof of her sincerity. Her constant and sincere grin connects with her admirers whether she is posing on the red carpet or interacting with them. Aniston's infectious charm and love for life are also reflected in her grin. It captures her excitement and young vitality, giving her an accessible and amiable air. She exudes enthusiasm and optimism with her grin, inviting people to partake in her happiness. It serves as a daily reminder of her capacity for joy and her ability to see the beauty in everything. Her grin also exudes a feeling of mystery and curiosity. It has a seductive aspect that draws onlookers in and makes them curious about the lady hidden behind the grin. She radiates warmth and openness, yet under the surface, there is a feeling of depth and complexity. Her grin adds a fascinating dimension to her identity as it alludes to layers of feelings and events that had formed her.

Throughout her career, Aniston has shown her grin both on and off the screen. Her grin has been a key component of her persona from her early days on "Friends" through her countless red-carpet outings and magazine covers. It has become a representation of her lasting beauty and charm after being captured in innumerable images.

In addition to being aesthetically pleasing, Aniston's grin has come to represent tenacity. It has endured personal hardships and media criticism, acting as a testament to her tenacity and capacity for perseverance. Many people who look to her as a role model for grace and optimism in the face of life's adversities find inspiration in her bright smile. Aniston's grin significantly changed popular culture and affected beauty ideals. Her recognizable grin and her "Friends" haircut have become sought-after features, influencing countless others all over the globe. Dentists have even seen a rise in patients asking for smiles like Jennifer Aniston's.

Finally, Jennifer Aniston's beaming grin has a charm that goes well beyond its aesthetic attractiveness. It embodies her sincerity, friendliness, and optimism and makes her accessible and relatable. Audiences are enthralled by her grin, which pulls them into her world and leaves a lasting impact. It is a representation of her vibrant personality and a source of strength and motivation. Jennifer Aniston's grin has a classic allure and mystique that never fails to charm and attract people throughout the globe.

Exposing Her Early Performing Experiences And Aspirations

The roots of enthusiasm and tenacity that grew into Jennifer Aniston's successful career may be seen in her early ambitions and experiences with performing. These formative years impacted her trajectory and put her on the road to celebrity, from her early acting ambitions through her early encounters in the business. Aniston has had a burning ambition to work as an actor since she was a little girl. She was exposed to the entertainment industry as a child and saw firsthand the rewards and hardships of the business. Aniston acquired a passion for performing and knew she wanted to make acting her job after being inspired by her father's acting career. She enrolled in the Fiorello H. LaGuardia High School of Music & Art and Performing Arts in New York City because she was passionate about acting. She received a formal education in the arts from this esteemed university, where she also had the opportunity to hone her trade. She devoted herself to taking a variety of acting lessons, developing her abilities, and mastering the methods that would later be useful to her in her profession.

She had a difficult time getting into the acting industry after graduating from high school. She started going to auditions, hoping to prove her potential and get her big break. As is typical for budding performers, these early interactions with the profession resulted in both successes and rejections. She had one of her first parts in the off-Broadway production of "For Dear Life." Despite the play's lack of broad acclaim, she gained vital experience from it and was able to hone her acting skills. Aniston continued to explore chances and hone her talents, demonstrating even at this early stage her commitment to her trade.

When she was cast in her first television role on the show "Molloy" in 1990, Aniston's perseverance paid off. Despite being brief, the program helped her career even if it was a stepping stone. Following that, she had some guest appearances on well-known television programs of the era, such as "Quantum Leap," "Herman's Head," and "Burke's Law." Aniston was able to garner recognition and demonstrate her acting flexibility thanks to her early television performances.

Aniston's life, however, altered irrevocably in 1994 when she was chosen to play Rachel Green in the wildly popular television sitcom "Friends." This part turned out to be her big break, propelling her into popularity on a global scale and making her one of the most famous and well-liked actors of her time. Audiences connected with Aniston's depiction of Rachel Green, a stylish and sympathetic girl, and it highlighted her comic timing and inherent charm.

Aniston's career was boosted by "Friends" fame, which also provided her with other opportunities in the film business. She started getting offers for prominent parts in films, enabling her to show off her flexibility outside of television. She demonstrated her ability to shift from television to cinema in early film roles in "She's the One," "Picture Perfect," and "The Object of My Affection," among other early works.

Aniston's early acting experiences and first objectives show how dedicated, passionate, and unwaveringly committed she is to her work. She steadily laid a strong basis for her future success via auditions, training, and persistently pursuing possibilities. She gained the foundation for the varied and talented actress she would become through her experiences in both television and movies during this formative time. The development of Jennifer Aniston from a young aspiring actress to an established celebrity throughout the world is evidence of her skill, tenacity, and unshakable commitment. Her early acting experiences and first objectives influenced her career and created the foundation for the spellbinding performances that made an enduring impression on the entertainment world.

CHAPTER 2

Information on Jennifer's Perseverance, Auditions, and Professional Successes

Jennifer Aniston's career is evidence of her unyielding tenacity, fortitude, and unceasing pursuit of her goals. Aniston's path is defined by her persistence and willingness to take chances, which finally helped her reach the peak of success in the entertainment world, from her early auditions to her professional achievements. Aniston had her fair share of auditions and rejections at the beginning of her career, just like many other aspiring performers. She maneuvered through Hollywood's cutthroat environment while perfecting her skills and looking for chances to show off her ability. Her perseverance was put to the test throughout these auditions as she dealt with the difficulties and uncertainties that come with the business.

Behind the smile

The tenacity of Aniston was immediately apparent. She demonstrated a strong work ethic and a love for her art when she went to auditions. She was aware that every chance, no matter how it turned out, was an opportunity for her to develop, grow, and improve as an actor. Aniston didn't let rejection stop her; instead, she used each setback as fuel to push forward and prove herself.

Throughout her career, Aniston has shown her tenacity and dedication to her work. She has consistently sought out hard and varied jobs, pushing herself to discover new acting genres. Aniston continuously proves her flexibility and commitment to her art, whether she's playing challenging roles in tragic movies or giving funny performances in comedy. Aniston has achieved success in acting, but she has also utilized her platform to support worthy causes and take part in charitable activities. She has participated in several charity organizations, lending her support to initiatives like cancer research, children's rights, and relief operations for natural disasters.

The success of Jennifer Aniston in her work is proof of the strength of grit, fortitude, and risk-taking. She has shown an unshakeable dedication to her profession throughout her path from auditions and early disappointments to her career achievements. Aniston's capacity for embracing difficulties, picking up lessons from mistakes, and continuing to develop as an actor has cemented her place among the most successful and adored individuals in the entertainment business.

Examining the influence and cultural relevance of "Friends"

The Role of a Lifetime: Rachel Green and the "Friends" Phenomenon

The enduring television comedy "Friends," which ran from 1994 to 2004, had a significant influence on pop culture and is still praised and adored by viewers all around the globe. The show's cultural importance goes well beyond its amusement value since it pioneered new concepts, addressed social concerns, and permanently altered the television industry.

"Friends" followed a group of six friends as they negotiated the ups and downs of life, love, and friendship in New York City: Rachel, Ross, Monica, Chandler, Joey, and Phoebe. The program resonated with viewers of all ages because it perfectly captured the spirit of the 1990s and spoke to the generation that was entering adulthood at the time.

The way "Friends" portrayed friendship was one of its most prominent features. Audiences all across the globe were moved by the main protagonists' close friendship and constant support for one another. The program praised friendship's strength and demonstrated how it can provide solace, hilarity, and a feeling of community. Many viewers developed strong bonds with the characters and felt as if they were a member of the "Friends" group themselves as a result of the show's resonant friendship concept.

Through its comedy and relatable plotlines, "Friends" had a big effect on pop culture. The program received praise from critics and fans alike for its deft writing, razor-sharp humor, and well-placed comedy moments. The show's catchphrases and inside gags, such as "How you doin'?" and "We were on a break," entered the vocabulary of popular culture and are still used today.

Beyond just being entertaining, "Friends" used a combination of comedy and empathy to address societal concerns. With a blend of humor and emotional depth, the program addressed issues of relationships, marriage, divorce, professional difficulties, and the problems of maturity. With its genuine depiction of the rewards and challenges of navigating maturity, it resonated with viewers who recognized themselves in the lives of the characters.

Behind the smile

The varied ensemble cast of "Friends" and its attempts to promote inclusion were also lauded. The program included characters from a variety of backgrounds and touched on issues of social acceptance, LGBTQ+ representation, and cultural diversity. The lack of ethnic diversity on the show drew criticism, but it's vital to recognize that "Friends" helped pave the way for more diverse storytelling in later television programs.

Beyond its first broadcast, "Friends" has had a significant influence. Even after it has ended, the program keeps attracting new viewers because of syndication, streaming services, and DVD releases. Its ongoing appeal is evidenced by its enduring comedy, likable characters, and overarching themes. Fans of many ages and backgrounds continue to find solace and happiness in rewatching "Friends" episodes, which have established the program as a cultural landmark.

Additionally, "Friends" has had a long-lasting impact on the television industry. Its popularity helped ensemble sitcoms to become popular and demonstrated the strength of an ensemble cast. Numerous other television shows have adopted and been affected by the structure and narrative strategies of the original program.

In summary, "Friends" has had a considerable influence on society at large and on television, holding a prominent position in popular culture. It attracted fans and has continued to touch viewers of all generations with its celebration of friendship, accessible tales, and balance of comedy and drama. The cultural relevance of "Friends" is found in its capacity to bring people together, start dialogues, and serve as a constant reminder of the worth of joy, love, and the everlasting strength of friendship.

CHAPTER 3

Examining Rachel Green as played by Jennifer and the show's continuing legacy

Many people consider Jennifer Aniston's depiction of Rachel Green in the popular television sitcom "Friends" to be one of her most famous and adored performances. Aniston's skill and charisma helped to bring Rachel's character arc to life, and it had a lasting impression on popular culture and viewers all over the globe. The relatability, development, and flawless chemistry of the whole cast are responsible for the show's long impact and Aniston's depiction of Rachel Green. In 1994, when "Friends" first aired, Rachel Green was presented as a young person who had lately eschewed an opulent existence in favor of forging her way in the world. Audiences were attracted by Aniston's depiction of Rachel's transformation from a self-absorbed and somewhat naïve young lady to a more independent, career-driven person. Rachel's fragility and tenacity were expertly matched by Aniston, giving the character depth and dimension. The fact that Rachel Green could relate to the audience was one of the main factors in her success. When it came to managing relationships, going after job aspirations, or dealing with the uncertainties of maturity, many individuals could identify with Rachel's experiences and difficulties. Rachel became charming and accessible because of Aniston's ability to imbue her with genuineness and sensitivity, winning over viewers of all ages. The character development of Rachel became more and more obvious as the series went on. She developed into a strong, independent person who was motivated to leave her imprint on the world from a young lady seeking her identity. Aniston expertly depicted Rachel's development on both a personal and professional level, guiding her through the challenges of dating, advancing in her work, and pursuing her aspirations.

Behind the smile

Aniston gave Rachel Green a lively vitality with her comic timing and innate wit. Aniston regularly added humor and brightness to the role, whether it was by delivering caustic one-liners, doing physical comedy, or demonstrating her amazing comic timing. The show's overall success and Rachel Green's continued popularity may be attributed to her ability to convey both comic and tragic moments with equal elegance. The chemistry among the ensemble cast of "Friends" was one of its defining characteristics, and Aniston's engaging interactions with her co-stars were crucial to the success of the program. One of the main plotlines of the series was the connection between Rachel and the other characters, especially her on-again, off-again romance with Ross (played by David Schwimmer). One of the most remarkable and lasting elements of the program was the on-screen chemistry between Aniston and Schwimmer as they portrayed Ross and Rachel's turbulent relationship.

Behind the smile

Beyond the original run of the program, "Friends" and Jennifer Aniston's depiction of Rachel Green continue to have a significant cultural impact. Years after it ended, "Friends" is still praised and adored by viewers all over the globe. The show's continued success is evidenced by obits ageless comedy, likable characters, and overarching themes.

The way that Aniston portrayed Rachel Green has permanently altered popular culture. The public is well-versed in her character's wardrobe choices, catchphrases, and personal stories "The Rachel," Rachel's signature hairdo, became well-known and inspired a global craze.

Furthermore, audiences of many generations continue to connect with the show's themes of friendship, love, and overcoming the difficulties of maturity. With new generations finding and enjoying "Friends" episodes via syndication and streaming services, the program has become a cultural icon.

Behind the smile

The role of Rachel Green that Jennifer Aniston played in "Friends" continues to be a turning point in her career. Millions of people were moved by her ability to give the character depth, sensitivity, and comedy, which cemented her reputation as an accomplished actor. Aniston's continuing brilliance and the significance of her depiction are shown by the success of "Friends" and the ongoing popularity of Rachel Green. Aniston's portrayal of Rachel Green not only demonstrated her acting prowess but also helped the program have a positive cultural influence and maintain its popularity.

The way "Friends" and Aniston's depiction of Rachel Green influenced popular culture is evidence of the show's effect. There are still allusions to the program in a variety of media, and the characters and their catchphrases have entered ordinary speech. The show's effect extends beyond simple entertainment, as it has changed how individuals dress, arrange their hair, and even see and manage their friendships.

Behind the smile

Audiences connected with Aniston's depiction of Rachel Green because she gave the role a feeling of realism and relatability. Moments of vulnerability, progress, and self-discovery dotted Rachel's path from a young lady establishing her independence to a strong, determined person. Because of the combination of warmth, comedy, and emotional depth that Aniston gave Rachel, she became a figure that viewers could identify with.

Furthermore, the success of the sitcom was greatly attributed to Aniston's chemistry with the rest of the ensemble. The performers' real friendship and camaraderie on-screen transferred into a fluid interaction between the roles. Aniston's relationships with her co-stars, who included Courteney Cox, Lisa Kudrow, Matt LeBlanc, Matthew Perry, and David Schwimmer, lent the show's depictions of friendships a feeling of reality and made them seem emotional and genuine.

Behind the smile

Another first for female characters on television was Aniston's depiction of Rachel Green. Independent, aspirational, and fearless in pursuing her goals, Rachel. Many young women looked up to her as a role model because she broke gender norms and encouraged them to follow their dreams, take charge of their lives, and value their uniqueness.

The influence of "Friends" and Jennifer Aniston's depiction of Rachel Green is also evident in the show's enduring appeal and relevancy. "Friends" has continued to be a cultural sensation even after it ended, bringing in new audiences via syndication, streaming services, and spin-offs. The show's friendship, love, and struggles of maturity themes have a timeless aspect that appeals to viewers of all ages.

Additionally, Aniston's depiction of Rachel Green has had a long-term effect on her professional life. It enhanced her reputation as a skilled performer and provided her with new possibilities. After "Friends," Aniston made a smooth move to the big screen, assuming a variety of parts that demonstrated her adaptability and acting talent.

Finally, Rachel Green's depiction by Jennifer Aniston in "Friends" has had a lasting impact on pop culture. The sitcom had a significant cultural influence and endured in popularity because of its ability to give the character realism, comedy, and emotional depth. Aniston's depiction of Rachel Green continues to strike a chord with viewers, and her performance is still seen as a turning point in her professional life. Because of the show's ageless themes and realistic experiences, "Friends" and its beloved heroine Rachel Green have achieved legendary status.

Jennifer's transition from Television to film

The fact that Jennifer Aniston was able to go smoothly from television to the big screen is a credit to her skill, adaptability, and flexibility. Aniston had a successful career in cinema after becoming well-known for her part as Rachel Green in the popular sitcom "Friends," displaying her versatility as an actor and establishing her position as a leading woman in Hollywood. Aniston wasted little time in making her imprint on the big screen once "Friends" ended in 2004. She purposefully selected a wide variety of cinema parts that gave her the freedom to depart from the comedy image and go into uncharted waters as an actor. A string of well-lauded performances that demonstrated her range and acting talent marked her move from television to movies.

Aniston portrayed Kate Mosley, the title character, in the romantic comedy "Picture Perfect," which was released in 1997. Aniston was able to showcase her charisma and comic timing in the movie, demonstrating that her abilities went beyond television. Even though "Picture Perfect" earned unfavorable reviews, it helped Aniston enter the movie business.

Aniston took on several parts at the beginning of her film career, which gave her the chance to experiment with various genres and display her acting versatility. She performed in comedies including "Office Space" (1999) and "The Object of My Affection" (1998), showcasing her talent for giving sharp and funny performances. Her reputation as a skilled comic actor was cemented by these parts, which also paved the way for other chances.

In 2003's romantic comedy "Bruce Almighty," Aniston had her breakthrough acting appearance with Jim Carrey. Her performance as Grace Connelly, a news reporter, and Carrey's love interest, solidified her position as a leading woman in the movie business. The success of "Bruce Almighty" underlined Aniston's ability to fascinate viewers in a larger-than-life theatrical setting in addition to showcasing her on-screen connection with Carrey. After she continued to build on her popularity, Aniston took on a variety of cinematic parts, showcasing her adaptability and desire to push herself as an actor. She co-starred with Ben Stiller in the romance drama "Along Came Polly" in 2004, displaying her versatility by handling more complex and emotionally charged roles. The success of the movie strengthened her reputation as a bankable leading woman.

In drama, like "The Good Girl" (2002), where she played a disillusioned retail worker looking for an escape from her mundane life, and "Marley & Me" (2008), a touching family movie where she co starred with Owen Wilson and a mischievous dog, Aniston has also given notable performances. Aniston was able to demonstrate her dramatic range in these roles and demonstrate her capacity for delivering intense performances. Aniston has experimented with different genres than romantic comedies and dramas, such as action comedies like "The Bounty Hunter" (2010) and ensemble comedies like "Horrible Bosses" (2011). Her repertoire was further diversified by these movies, which demonstrated her ability to deftly combine comedy with gripping performances.

Aniston's film career has been distinguished by favorable reviews, lucrative box office returns, and a steady presence in the business. In recognition of her efforts in "The Morning Show" (2019), she received a Screen Actors Guild Award for Outstanding Performance by a Female Actor in a Leading Role. She has received several nominations and awards for her work. Aniston has pushed boundaries and pursued new directions in her cinematic career recently. She received acclaim for her depiction of a lady suffering from chronic pain in the indie drama "Cake" (2014), which she both appeared in and executive produced. The part demonstrated Aniston's readiness to play complicated, difficult characters and her commitment to stretching the limits of her profession. Aniston had difficulties transitioning from television to the big screen. She had to deal with obvious parallels to her well-known "Friends" character Rachel Green, like many actresses switching across media. Aniston, however, has repeatedly shown that she is capable of eschewing the limitations of her television image and establishing herself as a flexible performer who can play a variety of parts.

In addition to her acting skills, Aniston's likability and screen presence have been crucial to her smooth transition to the big screen. Moviegoers love her for her inherent charisma, relatability, and capacity to connect with viewers. Her ability to give her characters depth and sincerity in comedies, dramas, and romance movies draws audiences. Aniston's transition from television to cinema has also shown her willingness to take chances and work with renowned filmmakers and other accomplished performers. She collaborated with well-known directors such as David O. Russell on "The Good Girl," Marlene Gorris on "The Diary of Anne Frank" (2009), and Nicole Holofcener on "Friends with Money" (2006). Aniston has been able to push herself and broaden her creative horizons thanks to these partnerships.

Behind the smile

Aniston has also shown her flexibility by pursuing projects both in front of and behind the camera, as well as by producing them. She worked as an executive producer on "The Morning Show," a highly praised television series, in addition to her job as an executive producer on "Cake," where she also had a strong performance. Her decision to go into producing is a reflection of her ambition to exercise creative freedom and contribute to the creation of engaging and thought-provoking tales. In addition to showcasing her skill and adaptability, Aniston's seamless move from television to cinema has cleared the way for other performers wishing to take a similar step. Her path acts as motivation for individuals wishing to leave behind a cherished television job and carve out a place for themselves in the cutthroat world of cinema.

In conclusion, Jennifer Aniston's transition from television to film is evidence of her brilliance, adaptability, and willpower. She has cemented her position as a leading woman in Hollywood with several varied roles and partnerships with renowned directors. Aniston is a versatile and well-liked actress because of her ability to enthrall viewers with her performances, whether in comedies, dramas, or romance movies. Her move from television to the cinema not only demonstrated her versatility but also provided opportunities for other actresses looking to take a similar step. Aniston keeps pushing boundaries, challenging herself, and making a mark on the movie business with each project she does.

Showcasing important cinema roles and the critical response

In her filmography, Jennifer Aniston has played several significant parts that have received critical praise and cemented her prestige as a skilled actor in Hollywood. She has continually given performances that have grabbed audiences and won praise from both reviewers and colleagues in everything from romantic comedies to tragedies.

Aniston played Justine Last, a disillusioned shop clerk caught in a loveless marriage, in the indie drama "The Good Girl" from 2002, one of her memorable early appearances. Critics praised Aniston's subtle and reflective performance and praised her ability to capture Justine's mental struggle and need for escape. In contrast to the humorous parts for which she had first achieved notoriety, her depiction revealed depth and variety. Nicole Holofcener's ensemble drama "Friends with Money," which examined the lives and relationships of four friends, starred Aniston as Olivia in 2006. Aniston received accolades for her portrayal of Olivia, a lady dealing with both emotional and financial difficulties. She further cemented her reputation as a skilled dramatic actor by receiving praise from critics for her ability to portray Olivia's inner turmoil and emotional journey. Aniston's role in the indie drama "Cake" in 2014 marked a turning point in her career. She portrays Claire Bennett, a character dealing with a personal tragedy and chronic suffering, in the movie. Aniston was able to demonstrate her acting talent and dedication in the part. Critics praised her for giving a "transformative performance," emphasizing how well she was able to convey the character's mental and emotional suffering. Aniston's role in "Cake" earned her praise from critics and nominations for several awards, including Best Actress at the Golden Globes. Aniston has succeeded in the romantic comedy genre in addition to her serious parts, winning over audiences all over the globe with her performances. In the 2004 movie "Along Came Polly," which starred Ben Stiller, she played one of her most cherished parts. Aniston is Polly Prince, a free-spirited lady who upsets the orderly lives of Stiller's character. She and Stiller received plaudits for their on-screen chemistry and humorous timing, and the movie was a financial success. Aniston became a sought-after actress in romantic comedies because of her ability to strike a balance between heart and wit.

Behind the smile

Aniston's romantic comedy "The Break-Up" (2006), in which she co-starred with Vince Vaughn, is another noteworthy example. Aniston's ability to convey both comic and emotional moments with realism was on full display in the movie, which addressed the complexity of a failed relationship. She received praise for her portrayal of Brooke Meyers from reviewers who noted her connection with Vaughn and her capacity to give the role nuance.

In movies like "Marley & Me" (2008), a touching family comedy-drama in which she co-starred with Owen Wilson, Aniston further demonstrates her range as an actor. Her depiction of a lady juggling the difficulties of marriage and training a wayward puppy struck a chord with viewers and demonstrated her talent for making an emotional connection. While Aniston has often gotten praise for her performances, she has also had some commercial success. Her comic skills and capacity to hold her own in an ensemble cast were on display in movies like "Horrible

Behind the smile

Bosses" (2011) and its follow-up, "Horrible Bosses 2" (2014). These movies did well at the box office, enhancing Aniston's reputation as a bankable celebrity. Aniston has received countless award nominations and awards throughout her career thanks to her performances. She has been honored by illustrious organizations including the Screen Actors Guild, Critics' Choice Movie Awards, and Golden Globe Awards. She has cemented her position as one of Hollywood's most admired and versatile actors because of her ability to switch between humorous and tragic parts with ease, as well as her on-screen charm and relatability.

Aniston's performances not only garnered positive reviews and financial success but also had a long-lasting effect on audiences and popular culture. Her sympathetic and engaging depictions of flawed but endearing characters in romantic comedies like "The Break-Up" and "Along Came Polly" have made her parts in those films memorable. Aniston is a favorite among viewers looking for a touching and realistic narrative because of her ability to convey compassion and sincerity in her performances. Aniston's performances have moreover constantly shown her breadth as an actor, from playing complicated and emotionally charged characters in dramas like "The Good Girl" and "Cake," to providing comic timing and wit in movies like "Marley & Me" and the "Horrible Bosses" series. Her adaptability has made it possible for her to take on a variety of roles and genres, guaranteeing that her career will always be exciting and surprising.

Aniston's contemporaries in the film business have taken note of her skill. She has received compliments for her professionalism, commitment, and spirit of cooperation on set. Her commitment to excellence and capacity to improve the performances of others around her have been praised by directors and co-stars. Aniston has gained the respect and admiration of her peers because of her dedication to her art and her willingness to take chances, thus confirming her status as a well-respected actress.

Aniston's star power, in addition to her performances, has aided ensemble films in their box office success. In movies like "The Bounty Hunter" (2010) and "Murder Mystery" (2019), where she appeared with performers like Gerard Butler and Adam Sandler, respectively, it was clear that she could fit into an ensemble cast and develop chemistry with her co-stars. Aniston's presence enhances these movies' sincerity and charm, raising the level of the group performances as a whole.

In addition to receiving positive reviews and enjoying economic success, Jennifer Aniston's film roles and performances have had a considerable impact on the cultural landscape. She has become a significant figure in the business because of the universal appeal of her likable and complex characters. Aniston's talent for bringing comedy, openness, and emotional depth to her performances has made a lasting impression on the movie business and solidified her standing as a cherished and admired actor.

In conclusion, Jennifer Aniston's filmography is distinguished by several crucial roles and favorable reviews. Her roles have continually shown her range, skill, and capacity to engage viewers in anything from romantic comedies to tragedies. Aniston's standing as a top actress in Hollywood has been cemented by her capacity to depict complicated and empathetic characters. Aniston's performances never fail to wow audiences and create a lasting impact, whether it is via her comic timing, emotional depth, or on-screen chemistry. Not only have her efforts in the film business garnered her praise and acclaim, but they have also had an impact on pop culture and how viewers see and value narrative on the big screen.

CHAPTER 4

Jennifer's personal hardships, Relationships, Heartbreak, and Triumph.

The public has often been interested in Jennifer Aniston's personal life as a well-known member of the entertainment business. She has been in high-profile partnerships throughout her career, and these relationships and personal problems have molded both her professional and personal path. Her marriage to fellow actor Brad Pitt is perhaps one of the most well-known elements of Aniston's personal life. The pair wed in a spectacular ceremony in July 2000 after meeting in 1998. They were regarded as one of Hollywood's most famous and gorgeous couples because of how widely their relationship was publicized. Aniston and Pitt did, however, announce their separation in 2005, and their divorce was formally completed the following year. It was a difficult and stressful period for Aniston as their divorce generated a lot of media attention and rumors. Aniston was subjected to increased public and media scrutiny surrounding her personal life after her divorce from Pitt. Several well-known actors, including Vince Vaughn, John Mayer, and Justin Theroux, were in her high-profile partnerships. Aniston's love entanglements and every action she took garnered attention in the media, which often examined her relationships. Aniston kept her cool and poised despite the continuous attention, concentrating on her career and personal development.

Aniston has had personal difficulties outside of her sexual partnerships. She has been candid about her struggles with body image and the demands of maintaining a certain image in the entertainment business. She has emphasized the value of self-acceptance and embracing one's uniqueness in interviews as she discusses the difficulties she had with body shaming and cultural expectations. Aniston has promoted self-love and acceptance via her platform and as a proponent of body positivity.

Aniston has also been open about her struggles with emotional stability and mental health. She has been candid about her struggles with self-doubt and worry, emphasizing the value of getting treatment and caring for one's mental health. Many of Aniston's admirers who may be going through similar difficulties have been touched by her openness to reveal her troubles and help break down the stigma associated with mental health concerns.

Behind the smile

Aniston has persevered and kept her attention on her job while facing personal challenges and being the subject of public scrutiny. She has won praise from critics for her work and has persisted in giving riveting performances. Her tenacity and willpower are evident in how she manages to juggle her personal and professional obligations.

Aniston has maintained her authenticity and groundedness throughout her personal experience, displaying grace and humor in the face of difficulty. She has advocated for key topics including women's empowerment and humanitarian endeavors using her platform. Aniston has supported charities including the Red Cross, Stand Up To Cancer, and St. Jude Children's Research Hospital via her charitable work.

In conclusion, high-profile romances, internal problems, and media scrutiny have all been a part of Jennifer Aniston's personal life. She has been the target of significant media scrutiny as a result of her divorce from Brad Pitt and subsequent personal relationships. Aniston has handled these difficulties, nevertheless, with elegance and resiliency, never losing sight of her professional and personal development. She has made use of her position to promote awareness of significant societal matters, including mental health and body image problems. Aniston is not only a skilled actor but also a role model for many thanks to her capacity to maintain honesty and promote good change.

Examining how she handled the media's Attention and became stronger

A tribute to Jennifer Aniston's fortitude, elegance, and unrelenting dedication to upholding her authenticity and personal well-being is her journey into the spotlight. She has been the subject of extensive media coverage, unending tabloid speculations, and ongoing personal life scrutiny since she is a well-known and adored personality in the entertainment business. Aniston has overcome these obstacles, proving to have a remarkable capacity for navigating the difficulties that come with celebrity.

Aniston's persistent emphasis on her personal pleasure and well-being is one of the fundamental factors in her capacity to endure public criticism. She has consistently underlined the value of prioritizing oneself and resisting pressure to meet social standards throughout her career. Aniston has made a point of expressing her dedication to self-acceptance, self-love, and personal development. She has stayed loyal to herself, following her hobbies and working on initiatives that are consistent with her principles and interests. She hasn't let the opinions of others influence her decisions.

Aniston has also shown a remarkable capacity for perseverance in the face of adversity and optimism. She has resisted getting involved in arguments in public or mudslinging despite the persistent rumors in the media and gossip columns. She has instead decided to concentrate on her career and surround herself with a network of adoring friends and family members. Aniston has been able to rise above the din and keep her composure by putting her personal pleasure and mental health first. Aniston has also honed a sharp sense of humor, which she uses as a potent weapon to counteract criticism and dispel rumors about her personal life. She has learned to laugh at herself and has shown her wit and charm in many interviews and public appearances. In addition to winning over followers, Aniston's ability to laugh at herself and not take herself too seriously serves as a reminder that she is just human and is capable of overcoming obstacles with resiliency and a grin.

Her emphasis on seclusion is a key component in Aniston's ability to handle media criticism. Despite being well-known, she has made an effort to limit undue interference in her private life. Aniston has established boundaries, keeping the amount of private material she divulges to the public to a minimum, and purposefully avoids social media. She intentionally keeps her private life apart from her public image to preserve her feeling of privacy and protect herself from unwarranted public attention.

Aniston has used her position to speak out on matters that are important to her and to fight for causes in addition to how she handles criticism from the public. She has influenced others by using her platform to promote mental health, women's empowerment, and body image concerns. Aniston has shown that she is devoted to changing the world by directing her efforts to activities that are good for the globe and that go beyond the sensational headlines.

In the end, Jennifer Aniston's capacity to endure criticism from the public and come out stronger is the consequence of her unshakable dedication to herself, her principles, and her personal development. Despite being the subject of frequent media attention, she has shown perseverance in the face of difficulty. Aniston

Behind the smile

has managed to avoid public scrutiny and maintain her status as a revered and adored person in the entertainment world because of her devotion to happiness, sense of humor, emphasis on privacy, and concentration on utilizing her platform for good. Her experience encourages others by showing the value of self-care, resiliency, and being true to oneself in the face of challenges from the outside world.

<u>Iconic Influence, Fashion, and Beauty:Jennifer's distinctive haircuts and sense of style throughout time</u>

Throughout her career, Jennifer Aniston has been known for setting trends and sporting classic haircuts. Aniston's wardrobe choices have shown her ageless elegance, carefree attitude, and ability to adjust to shifting trends while preserving her trademark look from her early days on "Friends" to her red-carpet appearances and beyond. Aniston rose to fame early in her career because of her portrayal of Rachel Green on the popular sitcom "Friends." Rachel's 90s-inspired dress choices gained a lot of attention and were extensively imitated by spectators. The "Rachel haircut," a layered, shoulder-length hairdo that instantly went viral, was made famous by Aniston's character. The haircut became a popular choice in hair salons all around the world since it matched Aniston's inherent beauty so well.

As her career developed, Aniston continued to hone her sense of style, moving away from Rachel Green's carefree, girl-next-door approach and toward a more refined and polished look. She favored traditional shapes, fitted clothing, and a simple color scheme that emphasized her innate beauty and ageless grace. As she continually exhibited elegance and refinement in her choice of designer dresses and stylish outfits, Aniston's red carpet appearances grew in anticipation.

Behind the smile

Aniston has long been known for her straightforward and adaptable sense of style. She favors simple shapes, fitted silhouettes, and understated jewelry so that her inherent beauty and self-assurance may shine. Aniston consistently retains an air of subtle elegance that has become her distinctive style, whether she chooses a sleek and fitted pantsuit, a figure-hugging little black dress, or a flowing bohemian-inspired gown.

Aniston's hairstyles have contributed significantly to shaping her distinctive image, in addition to her clothing choices. She experimented with many lengths and styles once the "Rachel" haircut became popular, displaying her adaptability and capacity to follow emerging trends. Aniston has had a variety of hairstyles throughout the years, from long, flowing locks to shorter, more angular styles. Numerous ladies all around the globe have been inspired by her haircuts, and she still sets trends with her always-changing hairstyles. Aniston's attitude toward clothing and hairstyles displays her self-assurance and honesty. She is not hesitant to try new things and experiment with her appearance, yet she never loses sight of her sense of classic elegance. Aniston has been recognized as a style icon as a result of her choices in clothing, which have appealed to both her followers and fashion connoisseurs. She has had a tremendous influence on the fashion industry in addition to her style. She has worked with fashion designers, been on the covers of prestigious publications, and been the inspiration for well-known fashion firms. Aniston has influenced trends and the way women see and embrace their particular style, which goes beyond her personal fashion choices.

In conclusion, Jennifer Aniston's enduring sense of style and signature hairdos have solidified her place as a style authority. Aniston has continually shown her ageless elegance, carefree style, and capacity to adjust to shifting trends via her wardrobe choices, from her first performances on "Friends" through her red carpet appearances and beyond. She has inspired innumerable ladies all over the globe with her effortless but stylish sense of style and flexibility in hairdos. Aniston's style decisions not only represent her taste but also have an impact on the larger fashion business, firmly establishing her status as a cherished fashion icon.

Examining her influence on society and aesthetic standards

There is no denying Jennifer Aniston's influence on cultural norms and beauty standards. She has questioned conventional beauty standards throughout her career, championed body acceptance, and changed how people see beauty. Aniston has become a recognizable name in the entertainment world because of her inherent beauty and sparkling smile. Her youthful charm and effortlessly stylish appearance have struck a chord with viewers all around the globe, motivating countless others to appreciate their inherent beauty. Aniston has established herself as a symbol of beauty that is both ageless and approachable because of her perfect skin, radiant complexion, and minimum use of makeup. Through her focus on self-acceptance and body positivity, Aniston has significantly impacted beauty standards. She has been transparent about her struggles with body image and has made use of her position to advocate for a healthy and holistic view of beauty. Aniston has spoken out against unattainable beauty standards and the demands to uphold a certain definition of perfection. She has motivated others to follow in her footsteps by enjoying her originality, loving her curves, and advocating self-love.

Aniston's influence on culture goes beyond just her looks. She has influenced society's attitudes and standards with her sympathetic on-screen roles and approachable presence. Aniston has played complex female characters that defy stereotypes and upend traditional narratives in a variety of roles, including her portrayal as Rachel Green on "Friends" and her extensive filmography. She has emphasized the depth and complexity of women via her performances, promoting a change in how women are depicted and understood in the media. Aniston's impact extends beyond her on-screen persona, too. She has promoted significant social causes and donated to philanthropic organizations using her notoriety and platform. She has worked with charities including the Red Cross, Stand Up To Cancer, and St. Jude Children's Research

Behind the smile

Hospital as part of her charitable endeavors. Aniston has shown that genuine beauty goes beyond outward attractiveness and includes compassion, generosity, and a dedication to having a good effect on the world by supporting these causes.

The fashion and beauty industries have also been impacted by Aniston's influence on cultural norms and beauty standards. Her enduring hairdos, including the "Rachel" haircut, set trends and prompted repeated trips to the hairdresser. She has become a style icon, and designers and fashion fans flock to her for inspiration because of her timeless and chic wardrobe choices. Aniston revolutionized what it means to be stylish by skillfully fusing elegance and simplicity, which has an impact on how people dress and carry themselves.

Additionally, Aniston's effect spans generations. She has become a recognizable character in popular culture due to her continuing relevance and broad appeal. She has a devoted following that crosses age divisions, demonstrating that her influence endures and connects with individuals from all walks of life.

In conclusion, Jennifer Aniston has had a significant and far-reaching influence on both beauty standards and popular culture. She has questioned accepted ideas of beauty and changed how society views and values uniqueness because of her inherent attractiveness, dedication to self-acceptance, and representation of varied and approachable individuals. Aniston has cemented her position as a key figure in popular culture through her support of body acceptance, her charitable work, and her impact on fashion and beauty trends. Her lasting influence has shaped beauty standards and encouraged people to value their distinctive beauty on the inside as much as the outside.

CHAPTER 5

Giving Back: Activism and Philanthropy

Jennifer's commitment to humanitarian issues and charity initiatives

One of the most important facets of Jennifer Aniston's public character has been her commitment to humanitarian issues and charity endeavors. She has constantly had a good influence on the world and supported many charitable causes throughout her career by using her platform and resources. The battle against cancer is one of the noteworthy issues Jennifer Aniston has supported. She has been a strong supporter of groups like Stand Up To Cancer and has been an outspoken champion of cancer research and treatment. Aniston has taken part in several charity events and telethons to promote awareness of and raise money for cancer research. Her engagement has significantly increased awareness of the issue and public support, resulting in improvements in patient care and cancer treatment. Additionally, Aniston has been actively interested in causes that promote the welfare of children. She has long supported St. Jude Children's Research Hospital, which treats children with life-threatening diseases regardless of their family's financial situation. Aniston has visited the hospital and taken part in fundraising activities to cheer up the young patients while also earning money for their care and treatment. Her commitment to helping underprivileged children has made a significant difference in the lives of numerous families.

Aniston has shown her support for humanitarian groups and relief efforts in response to many humanitarian situations. She has worked on initiatives for the Red Cross, an organization that offers immediate aid during global humanitarian crises and natural catastrophes. Aniston's advocacy work and fundraising initiatives have aided in increasing awareness and giving those in need emergency supplies.

Behind the smile

Aniston has also committed to championing social causes and raising public awareness of crucial topics. She has lobbied for environmental protection, women's emancipation, and gender equality using her influence. Aniston has offered her voice to movements and projects that seek to make society a better place. She is a reputable change agent due to her dedication to social justice and her readiness to speak up about these concerns.

Aniston is committed to helping others in ways other than via monetary contributions and public appearances. She has actively participated in practical charity, going to the impacted areas herself and utilizing her platform to raise awareness of their issues. Her sincere empathy and concern for others have impacted the lives of individuals she has dealt with and motivated others to take action to change the world.

Aniston has also used her notoriety and status to encourage and uplift other artists. She has participated in humanitarian projects in the entertainment sector including the SAG-AFTRA Foundation, which helps and supports artists in need. Aniston's determination to leverage her platform for the greater good is shown by her loyalty to her coworkers and her readiness to support the arts community.

In conclusion, Jennifer Aniston's commitment to humanitarian issues and endeavors is evidence of her caring and giving character. She has significantly impacted the lives of many people via her support of many organizations and active engagement in fundraising and advocacy. Aniston's dedication to enhancing children's lives, assisting with cancer research, and supporting significant social concerns has established her as a reputable philanthropist and humanitarian. She inspires others and exemplifies her unshakable commitment to changing the world for the better through her real compassion, hands-on engagement, and use of her platform to raise awareness and assistance for those in need.

Jennifer Anniston's support for mental health and women's empowerment

Jennifer Aniston has been a strong supporter of women's rights and mental health, utilizing her position to raise awareness of these vital problems and encourage progress. Her advocacy work has had a huge influence in these areas, encouraging and empowering women all over the globe and dispelling stigmas associated with mental health. Aniston is a well-known member of the entertainment world who often advocates for women's empowerment and gender equality. She has discussed the difficulties faced by women in the field, such as the representation and salary gaps between the sexes. Aniston has fought for greater inclusion and portrayal of women both in front of and behind the camera. She has been a passionate proponent of equal opportunity and fair treatment for women. Beyond her career in the entertainment business, Aniston is an advocate. She has taken a leading role in promoting women's rights and empowerment via groups like Equality Now. She has contributed to increasing awareness of the value of gender equality and the need to build a more inclusive and fair society by supporting and taking part in events and initiatives. Aniston has been an outspoken supporter of destigmatizing mental illness in addition to her work for women's rights. She has been transparent in discussing her struggles with anxiety and despair as well as other mental health issues. Aniston has aided in removing obstacles and promoting open discussions about mental health by sharing her experience. Aniston has made use of her position to promote self-care, increase awareness about the value of getting treatment, and normalize conversations about mental health. She has urged people to prioritize their mental health and to get help when they need it via interviews, lectures, and social media postings. Because of Aniston's openness to talk freely and honestly about her troubles, other people have been motivated to do the same, creating a feeling of solidarity and community among others who are dealing with mental health issues.

Aniston has also worked on initiatives to raise awareness of mental health concerns and to provide support to mental health organizations. For instance, she provided the narration for the documentary "Bipolar Rock 'N Roller," which explores the experiences of a sportscaster who has bipolar illness. As a result of Aniston's engagement in these initiatives, there is a greater awareness of and sympathy for individuals who suffer from mental health issues. Aniston's commitment to supporting mental health awareness and women's empowerment has had a significant influence on people all around the globe. Destigmatizing mental health issues and promoting an open and caring culture has been made possible by her genuineness and readiness to utilize her own experiences to instruct and inspire others. Aniston has inspired women to speak up, accept their uniqueness, and chase their aspirations via her advocacy activities. She has also been instrumental in building understanding and empathy, promoting self-care, and bringing attention to issues related to mental health.

In conclusion, Jennifer Aniston has made mental health and women's empowerment a big part of her public character. She has fought for gender equality using her platform, questioned traditional standards, and backed groups that defend women's rights. Aniston's candor about her struggle with mental illness has also contributed to the reduction of stigma and increased awareness of mental illness. Her commitment to these issues has had a big effect, motivating and empowering people while promoting honest dialogue and constructive change. Aniston's advocacy activity is evidence of her dedication to changing the world and utilizing her platform to promote justice and compassion.

CHAPTER 6

The Influence of Resistance and Innovation

Jennifer's capacity to overcome obstacles and take up new ones

Jennifer Aniston's capacity to overcome obstacles and take on new ones is evidence of her tenacity, tenacity, and unrelenting spirit. She has had hurdles and disappointments throughout her work and personal life, but she has repeatedly shown the capacity to rise above adversity and succeed in the face of difficulties.

The 2004 finale of the cherished sitcom "Friends" was one of Aniston's career's most prominent disappointments. She had established herself as Rachel Green, and the program had amassed a sizable fan base. Many questioned whether Aniston would be able to leave the role that had defined her for ten years with success. She, however, welcomed the chance for development and actively sought out new difficulties.

Following the conclusion of "Friends," Aniston entered the film business and took on a variety of parts that demonstrated her range as an actor. Even while not all of her film efforts were as successful as "Friends," she persisted and kept looking for jobs that would stretch her artistically. Aniston exhibited her dedication to progress and her reluctance to be constrained by prior accomplishments by being ready to take chances and push herself beyond her comfort zone.

Aniston has had personal difficulties in addition to professional losses. When she and actor Brad Pitt publicly separated in 2005, she had to deal with tremendous media attention and public rumor. She nonetheless put her attention on herself and directed her energies into her career and personal development. Many people have found encouragement in Aniston's ability to handle personal challenges with grace and resiliency since it shows her strength and willpower to move on.

Aniston's fortitude and capacity to overcome obstacles also apply to her private life. She has been candid about the demands of celebrity, self-doubt, and body image difficulties. She has developed into a supporter of self-acceptance, self-care, and accepting one's real self as a result of her path of self-discovery and personal development. Fans have responded favorably to Aniston's candor and openness in exposing her hardships, which has encouraged others to meet their obstacles head-on and with fortitude.

Additionally, Aniston's ongoing exploration of various roles and projects demonstrates her readiness to take on new challenges. She has taken on a variety of genres and roles, demonstrating her acting ability and aptitude. Aniston continuously pushes herself to broaden her range and take on jobs that test the limits of her ability, whether it's in tragic roles like

Behind the smile

"Cake" or hilarious performances in movies like "Horrible Bosses."

Aniston's tenacity and optimistic outlook are the foundation of her capacity to overcome obstacles and rise to new ones. She can overcome challenges and consistently reinvent herself because of her strong work ethic and dedication to personal progress. Her career and success in the entertainment business have been largely attributed to her capacity to adjust to shifting conditions and grab new possibilities.

Jennifer Aniston's capacity to overcome obstacles and take on new ones is a testament to her fortitude, tenacity, and unrelenting spirit. She has experienced professional losses, personal difficulties, and severe public scrutiny, yet she has constantly shown the fortitude to triumph over obstacles and seize new possibilities. Aniston has developed as an actor and continues to be an inspiration to others because she is ready to go outside of her comfort zone, take chances, and push herself artistically. Her experience serves as a reminder that failures are not the end but rather provide chances for development and change.

Examining her ventures into producing and directing as well as broadening her artistic horizons

The artistic trajectory of Jennifer Aniston has not just included acting. She has dabbled with producing and directing throughout the years, broadening her views beyond the limitations of the screen. Her explorations into various areas have shown her creativity, ambition, and diversity. Aniston's interest in producing came to be as a result of her career's natural growth. To create and produce intriguing film and television projects, she co-founded the production firm Echo Films in 2008. Aniston has deliberately searched out narratives that speak to her and empower overlooked voices via Echo Films. She has contributed to the production of works including "The Switch," "Cake," and the highly acclaimed "Dumplin'," which was praised for its body-positive message and energizing narrative.

Aniston has added directing to her list of duties in addition to producing. In 2006, as a part of the anthology film "Five," she made her directing debut with the short film "Room 10." The movie examined the lives of people impacted by breast cancer and demonstrated Aniston's dedication to bringing attention to significant social concerns. Her directing job showcased her narrative skills and signaled the beginning of a new stage in her creative development. Aniston has also broadened her artistic boundaries by investigating options in other fields. She has dabbled in the cosmetics and fragrance industries, working with companies to create her line of trademark smells. Her engagement in the development of these scents is a reflection of her ambition to develop a deeper connection with her audience and explore new modes of self-expression.

Behind the smile

Aniston has been able to take more influence over her projects and experiment with various areas of narrative thanks to her forays into producing, directing, and other creative efforts. She has positioned herself as a creative force behind the scenes and broadened her impact beyond performing by taking on these tasks.

Aniston has also shown her dedication to supporting various stories and perspectives with her endeavors in producing and directing. She has aggressively sought out projects that highlight marginalized viewpoints and give budding talent a chance. Aniston's commitment to diversity and her desire to produce relevant and genuine material has struck a chord with both viewers and business leaders.

She has gained notoriety and appreciation as a result of her growth in these creative professions. For her work on the movie "Cake," Aniston was nominated for a Producers Guild of America Award, demonstrating her skill as a producer. Her work as a director in "Room 10" was also favorably praised, further solidifying her reputation as a multi-talented artist who can thrive in a variety of artistic capacities. Aniston has shown her ability to push the limits of her artistic talents by dabbling in producing, directing, and other creative pursuits. Her flexibility and commitment to growing as an artist are shown by her ability to jump into these roles with assurance and success.

In conclusion, Jennifer Aniston has shown her flexibility and ambition outside of acting via her pursuit of producing, directing, and broadening her creative horizons. She has supported marginalized voices via her production firm and created projects that speak to her. Her ability to convey a compelling tale and dedication to bringing attention to pressing social problems have been highlighted through her work as a filmmaker. Through her forays into these fields, Aniston has grown in stature and been recognized as a creative force in the business. She keeps inspiring people and securing her reputation as a multidimensional artist by taking on new challenges and pursuing novel creative outlets.

Life Lessons from Jennifer Aniston's Story

Jennifer Aniston's career in the entertainment business has been rich with insightful observations and life lessons that may motivate and strike a chord with people from all backgrounds. Here are some important lessons we may learn from her path, from her early challenges to her extraordinary success:

1.) The ability to persevere in the face of difficulty: Aniston's path is proof of the strength of persistence. Early in her career, she experienced rejection and failures, but she never gave up on her goals. She is an encouragement to never give up on our ambitions, even when the road looks difficult because of her tenacity to overcome challenges and keep moving ahead.

2.)Taking advantage of development opportunities: Aniston's capacity to accept new challenges and broaden her horizons emphasizes the value of moving outside of our comfort zones. She continually sought jobs that challenged her, and to explore many facets of her creativity, she also tried her hand at producing and directing. This reminds us of the importance of seizing chances for both personal and professional development, even when they appear challenging or uncharted.

3. The ability to bounce back from criticism: Throughout her career, Aniston has been the target of criticism and public scrutiny. She has grown a thick skin, however, and has stuck to her principles. Her capacity to overcome hardship and maintain her authenticity serves as a reminder to us of the value of being rooted in our truth.

4.) It is Good to Multitask: Aniston has managed the difficulties of keeping a great job while simultaneously giving her personal life priority. She has shown the value of maintaining a balance between professional and personal ties, prioritizing self-care, and setting aside time for the people and things that are genuinely important.

5.) Total Acceptance of Oneself: Aniston has openly discussed her path towards self-acceptance and has spoken in favor of accepting one's genuine self. Many people may relate to her message of self-acceptance and love, which serves as a reminder to value our individuality and accept our flaws.

6.) Giving back and making a difference: Aniston's commitment to advocacy work and philanthropic initiatives emphasizes the significance of giving back to the community and leaving a lasting impression. Her engagement in several charitable projects shows us the importance of utilizing our influence and resources to help causes that are important to us.

7.) The strength of flexibility and resilience: This is shown by Aniston's capacity to reinvent herself and succeed in a variety of roles and media. She has shown that it is never too late to discover new interests and career options, encouraging us to consider how reinventing oneself may result in exciting chances and personal development.

8.) Authenticity and being loyal to oneself: Aniston has maintained her integrity and stayed faithful to her principles throughout her career. Her dedication to maintaining her sense of self-awareness and groundedness serves as a reminder to put authenticity first in all facets of life.

To sum up, Jennifer Aniston's path gives insightful perspectives and life lessons that may motivate and direct us. Her experience shows us the value of patience, accepting new difficulties, resilience, juggling professional and personal obligations, self-acceptance, charitable giving, resilience, and self-reinvention. We may manage our paths with elegance, tenacity, and honesty by accepting these teachings, which will eventually lead to our finding both personal and professional satisfaction.

Motivating readers to follow their goals, accept their authenticity, and get past challenges

Readers may draw strength from Jennifer Aniston's inspiring path to follow their goals, embrace honesty, and overcome challenges in their own lives. She has shown the value of resiliency, self-belief, and being true to oneself via her experiences. Following are some ways her tale might encourage and inspire readers:

1. Dream-chasing without fear or hesitation: Aniston's path serves as a powerful example of the importance of dream-chasing without fear or doubt. She took chances, dealt with rejection, and persisted in her quest for an acting profession. Her narrative inspires readers to discover their interests and fully follow them despite any difficulties that may come along.

2. Embracing honesty: Throughout her career, Aniston's dedication to authenticity has served as a compass. She hasn't compromised her ideals or stayed loyal to herself to fit in with society's standards. Readers may discover the confidence to be their real selves, exhibit their special gifts, and accept their uniqueness by embracing authenticity.

3. Resilience in the face of adversity: Aniston's road is littered with innumerable challenges, disappointments, and rejections. However, she has continuously shown resilience by recovering from setbacks and continuing in the face of difficulties. Readers discover the value of resiliency and how to see setbacks as chances for development and learning from her tale.

4. Believing in oneself despite criticism and skepticism from others: Aniston never let her self-confidence waver. She had confidence in herself and her abilities, which eventually helped her succeed. Readers are reminded by her

persistent self-belief that having faith in one's skills is crucial for accomplishing one's objectives.

5. Accepting failures as stepping-stones to success: Jennifer Aniston's story is proof that setbacks and failures are not indicators of one's potential but rather occasions for development. Early in her career, she had rejections and setbacks, but she utilized them as stepping stones to advance. This viewpoint may encourage readers to see mistakes as useful lessons that eventually help them grow personally and professionally.

6. Aniston's narrative exhorts readers to consider their own personal pleasure and contentment. She has stressed the value of self-care, balance, and cultivating meaningful connections despite her enormous success. Readers are motivated to link their objectives with their principles to live a full and well-rounded life that goes beyond professional success.

7. Aniston's journey serves as a reminder that cultural constraints and expectations shouldn't influence one's choices or define their value. Resisting societal demands and choosing one's path. She has broken through boundaries, disproved prejudices, and carved herself her niche in the business. The book exhorts its audience to defy social conventions, trust their instincts, and live lives loyal to their own goals and objectives.

In conclusion, Jennifer Aniston's motivational tale encourages readers to follow their passions, value honesty, and overcome challenges. Her experience serves as an example of the strength of resiliency, self-belief, and being loyal to oneself. Readers may learn the confidence to pursue their interests, be true to themselves, and forge their pathways with persistence and elegance by taking after her example. Readers are inspired by Aniston's narrative, which serves as a reminder that everything is achievable with hard work, determination, and self-confidence.

CHAPTER 7

Legacy and Upcoming Projects

Analyzing Jennifer's long-term effects on the entertainment sector

There is no disputing Jennifer Aniston's influence on the entertainment business. She has developed into a legendary character throughout her career, having an impact on both the acting industry and popular culture in general. Here, we look into her impact's numerous facets:

1. Aniston's depiction of Rachel Green in the popular TV series "Friends" significantly contributed to the comedy genre's redefinition. Her endearing and likable persona, along with her perfect comic timing, contributed to "Friends" becoming a worldwide hit. The success of the program not only propelled Aniston to fame but also established new benchmarks for group humor and the

representation of complicated relationships on television.

2. Aniston's sense of style has had a significant effect on popular culture and fashion, setting trends in both categories. With her haircuts, outfit selections, and general aesthetic influencing trends in the '90s and beyond, her character Rachel Green became a fashion icon. The "Rachel" hairdo went viral, and Aniston's red carpet outfits continue to be a source of inspiration for fashion lovers. She has cemented her position as a timeless fashion star with her effortless, stylish look.

3. Breaking the "TV to film" stigma: Aniston overcame the stereotype that often surrounds performers known largely for their TV performances by leaping television to the big screen. With memorable roles in movies like "Marley & Me," "The Break-Up," and "Horrible Bosses," she demonstrated her flexibility and established herself as a bankable film actor. Her smooth transition made it easier for other

performers to make the shift from television to movies.

4. Increasing the status of women in the industry: Aniston has actively promoted gender equality in Hollywood. She has aggressively fought for improved chances and representation for women in the business, speaking out against sexism in the process. Her work has sparked crucial discussions about gender parity that have resulted in improvements and increased visibility for women in front of and behind the camera.

5. Humanitarian work and philanthropy: Aniston's dedication to these issues has had a profound effect outside of the entertainment sector. She has participated in several humanitarian endeavors, supporting groups dedicated to cancer research, children's welfare, and emergency assistance. Her advocacy work has brought attention to significant social concerns and motivated others to utilize their platforms for good.

6. Aniston is an inspiration to future generations of performers because of her brilliance, longevity, and capacity for self-reinvention. Her transformation from a struggling actress to a successful and well-liked celebrity is proof of the value of endurance, hard work, and drive. She has been praised as a role model by several actresses, who are inspired by her adaptability, honesty, and capacity to engage audiences.

7. Jennifer Aniston's name has come to be associated with skill, elegance, and enduring appeal. Iconic stature and cultural legacy. She has cemented her status as an icon whose impact continues to reverberate with audiences of all ages thanks to her contributions to the entertainment industry. She has earned a spot in pop cultural history because of the ongoing success of "Friends" and her subsequent cinematic endeavors.

The entertainment business has been significantly and long-lastingly impacted by Jennifer Aniston. She has permanently impacted popular culture with her endearing characters, classic aesthetic, and dedication to charity. She empowers women, motivates performers, and changes how we see comedy, fashion, and the business as a whole. Her effect goes beyond the screen. For many years to come, Jennifer Aniston's impact as an actor, style icon, and philanthropist will continue to inspire and reverberate.

The Everlasting Spirit of Jennifer Aniston.

The path Jennifer Aniston has taken in the entertainment business is evidence of her tenacious character, resiliency, and unrelenting commitment to her work. Aniston has captivated audiences all over the globe with her skill, charisma, and honesty, from her early difficulties as a young actor to her breakthrough role in "Friends" and her subsequent success in cinema and television.

Behind the smile

Aniston has handled the ups and downs of the business gracefully throughout her career, always reinventing herself and taking on new challenges. She has repeatedly shown that she is not afraid to go outside of her comfort zone by accepting a variety of roles and experimenting with other genres. Her smooth switch between comic and serious performances demonstrates both her flexibility and dedication to improving her art.

Beyond her on-screen successes, Aniston has also made a difference in the world by using her platform to promote significant causes. She has taken an active role in charity, lending assistance to groups and projects that are concerned with disaster relief, children's welfare, and cancer research. Her commitment to helping others demonstrates her understanding and care for them. Aniston stands out not just for her brilliance but also for her unpretentiousness and relatability. She has consistently stayed loyal to herself, refusing to compromise her ideals or act following social norms. She has won over admirers all around the globe because of her approachability and down-to-earth demeanor, making her a well-liked figure in the business.

We are reminded of the importance of tenacity, self-belief, and being true to oneself as we think back on Jennifer Aniston's lasting spirit. Her path serves as motivation for anyone pursuing their ambitions and aspirations, including budding performers. She has encountered obstacles and failures, but she has always come out stronger by seeing each situation as a chance for development.

Aniston has had a significant effect on the entertainment business, and her legacy will continue to have an impact on future generations. She had a lasting impression on popular culture via her portrayals of well-known characters, her contributions to fashion and style, and her dedication to charity. She has dismantled barriers, disproved preconceptions, and made it possible for other performers to pursue their passions.

Finally, Jennifer Aniston personifies the tenacity of a great artist. Her place as an icon in the entertainment business has been cemented by her skill, tenacity, and sincerity. We can anticipate her to make a lasting impression and continue to inspire others with her unrelenting enthusiasm and devotion as she develops and pursues new professional opportunities. The life story of Jennifer Aniston is a tribute to the strength of tenacity, honesty, and pursuing one's goals.

The lasting impact she leaves behind

The lasting impact Jennifer Aniston leaves behind in the entertainment world, together with her skill and resiliency, make her a great example for others. Her extraordinary journey and accomplishments have forever changed Hollywood and continue to inspire people all across the globe. Her tenacity is one of Aniston's most notable traits. She has had many obstacles and disappointments during her career, but she has always been able to overcome them and come back even stronger. Aniston has shown unshakable tenacity and endurance in following her love for acting, overcoming early rejections and challenges to achieve breakthrough successes and critical acclaim. Her capacity for overcoming challenges is a potent reminder that failures do not determine one's value and that, with resiliency and determination, one may accomplish their goals.

Aniston has acting skills. She has consistently provided nuanced and intriguing representations, beginning with her debut role as Rachel Green in "Friends" and continuing with her riveting turns in movies like "The Good Girl," "Marley & Me," and "Cake." She demonstrates her flexibility and range as an actor by switching between humor and drama with ease. Aniston is a well-liked and recognized figure in the business because of her inherent charm, perfect comic timing, and capacity to portray nuanced emotions. Jennifer Aniston leaves a wide-ranging and lasting impact. Her role as Rachel Green in "Friends" has first and foremost become a legendary cultural symbol. Aniston's position in television history has been cemented by the show's enormous success and ongoing significance. She became a favorite of the audience because of the appeal of her character Rachel and her comic timing. Aniston's depiction as Rachel Green has continued to enthrall new generations of fans via repeats and streaming services even years after the show's conclusion.

The influence of Aniston goes beyond "Friends" as well. Her ability and adaptability are shown by the success of her transfer from television to movies. She has assumed a variety of roles, demonstrating her versatility in handling various personalities and genres. Aniston regularly gives performances that connect with viewers and reviewers, whether they are in serious dramas like "The Morning Show" or romantic comedies like "The Break-Up."

Behind the smile

Furthermore, it is impossible to ignore Aniston's impact on beauty and fashion. She has become a fashion star and trendsetter thanks to her ageless style, recognizable haircuts, and natural attractiveness. The "Rachel" hairdo of the 1990s and Aniston's red-carpet outfits are just a few examples of how her fashion choices have had a lasting impression on society. Numerous admirers and fashion aficionados have been impressed by her easy grace and ability to make any clothing appear elegant.

Aniston's humanitarian activities and advocacy work are further evidence of her compassion and commitment to having a good influence. She has supported several philanthropic organizations and has used her position to spread the word about and promote vital causes including mental health, children's welfare, and cancer research. Her dedication to helping others and making a difference is a perfect example of what makes a caring and powerful person.

Behind the smile

In conclusion, it is worthwhile to celebrate Jennifer Aniston's tenacity, skill, and long impact on the entertainment world. She has become an icon and an inspiration to many because of her capacity to overcome obstacles, her prodigious acting abilities, and her influence on popular culture. Her legacy will continue to inspire the next generations of performers, artists, and anyone working to achieve their aspirations with passion, tenacity, and sincerity. Aniston made immeasurable contributions to television, cinema, fashion, and charity.

Printed in Great Britain
by Amazon

36185246R00059